Quality

in the
Public Sector

Essential Skills for the Public Sector

PUBLICATIONS

Jennifer Bean
Lascelles Hussey

HB PUBLICATIONS
(Incorporated as Givegood Limited)

Published by:

**HB Publications
London, England**

British Library Cataloguing in Publication Data

ISBN 1899448 06 3

Printed and bound in England by Short Run Press Limited Exeter

Contents

Chapter 1

INTRODUCTION

In todays environment, quality is a major issue for all organisations striving towards continuous improvement. Quality issues have become extremely important in the public sector, as Central Government is placing increasing emphasis on the quality of outputs and outcomes from public services. Public sector managers are tasked with the responsibility of delivering high quality services within tight financial constraints and, therefore, obtaining the best possible value for money services.

The key questions facing managers with respect to quality are:

- ❖ How do we define it? (Particularly as some public sector services are intangible in nature.)
- ❖ How do we measure it? and
- ❖ How do we monitor it?

These questions are complicated by the need to become more customer focused, as views on quality are not the sole domain of those delivering the service, but also those receiving it.

Managers need to equip themselves with the skills and knowledge to develop appropriate quality standards for the services they deliver. This books seeks to assist in the development of these skills and knowledge and outlines practical tools that can be used to answer many of the key questions about quality in relation to public sector services.

It is increasingly common for public sector organisations to seek recognition for having a quality service and there are a number of quality kite marks that can be achieved. This books sets out what is needed in order to achieve the most popular of these kite marks, and how the process should be applied in a public sector setting.

This book will also address the common problem of trying to maintain or improve quality standards in a climate of constrained or shrinking financial resources.

The principles described in this book are often illustrated with practical examples and can be applied to most public sector services. Self development questions are given at the end of each chapter to allow the reader to consider how the techniques discussed can be applied to specific service areas within their organisation. This book seeks to demystify many of the issues surrounding quality in the public sector and assist managers in working towards the delivery of high quality services.

Chapter 2

WHAT IS QUALITY?

Defining Quality

Quality is extremely important for the public sector and is a term that is used frequently with respect to public sector services. Quality is often used in the context of:

- ❖ Establishing value for money
- ❖ Setting quality thresholds for service provision
- ❖ Creating an image
- ❖ Public perception
- ❖ Service specification

Quality, by its very nature, is subjective and will mean different things to different people. It is also accepted that there are different levels of quality. Hence, defining quality in a general way is virtually impossible.

Despite the difficulties with definitions, there exist a number of standardised definitions of quality. The most familiar are as follows:

"Quality is conformance to requirements"
Philip B Crosby - Quality is Free

"Quality means that your product should be fit for its intended purpose"
Kit Sadgrove - ISO 9000 Made Easy

"Quality is a degree of excellence"
Concise Oxford Dictionary 9th Edition

Many authors do not try to define quality, but treat quality as a concept which is interpreted by individuals and organisations with respect to different goods and services.

What is clear is that quality needs to be defined if it is to be understood in the same way by everybody. In this book we will seek to identify the types of factors that influence the quality definition that will be developed by an organisation or manager with respect to their services. Understanding these factors will help to ensure the most appropriate quality definition is used for the organisation and service in question.

The types of factors which influence quality include:

a) The strategic objectives of the organisation with respect to service provision

b) The organisational value systems

c) Consumer attitudes and expectations

d) Employees attitudes and expectations

e) The market place

f) The communication methods being applied

Each of these factors are discussed further as follows:

Strategic objectives with respect to the provision of services

❖ Purpose of the service

■ *Long lasting*

■ *Investment*

■ *Life enhancement*

■ *Re-cycling*

■ *Prevention*

■ *Cure*

■ *Protection*

■ *Value added*

■ *Enforcement*

■ *Customer satisfaction*

❖ There may be one or a combination of different service objectives that need to be achieved

Organisational value systems

❖ Usually represented by policies on issues such as:

■ *Equality*

■ *Customer care*

■ *Health and safety*

■ *Environment*

■ *Profitability*

■ *Accountability*

■ *Social/community responsibility*

❖ The policies may in some cases conflict with one another leading to a confused value system

Consumer attitudes and expectations

The consumers of products and services may assume the following:

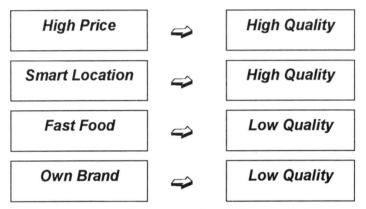

High Price	⇨	High Quality
Smart Location	⇨	High Quality
Fast Food	⇨	Low Quality
Own Brand	⇨	Low Quality

❖ These assumptions may be influenced by a range of external factors such as:

- *Family/home environment*

- *Friends/peers*

- *Work environment*

- *Public opinion*

- *Past experience*

- *Media*

- *Image*

❖ The consumers perception of quality will be affected by their own attitude and expectation.

❖ In formulating the quality definition, the most common consumers attitudes and expectations need to be taken into account.

Employee Attitudes and Expectations

❖ The quality definition, particularly in the public sector, should be strongly affected by employees attitudes and expectations. It is they who deliver the service and interpret how the organisation's values are put into practice.

❖ This interpretation and implementation process is often determined by the employee's own set of influences which are the same as those listed for the consumer.

The Market Place

❖ The nature of the market place affects the quality definition, in particular with respect to what is considered high and low quality.

❖ The market place may be characterised in a number of ways, including the following:

- *Monopoly*

- *Oligopoly*

- *Cartel operations*

- *High number of suppliers*

- *Low number of suppliers*

- *High level of demand*

- *Low level of demand*

- *High cost of entry*

- *Low cost of entry*

For example, in the case of a market place where there is a high number of suppliers, competition will affect the quality definition – usually leading to higher levels of quality as competitors try to gain a competitive edge.

Communication Methods Being Applied

❖ Everyone's understanding of quality varies and is often dependent upon the messages that are communicated about the service and the communication method used

❖ Communication methods may be:

- *Written*

- *Visual*

- *Verbal*

using a range of techniques such as publicity, literature, video, television, radio, word of mouth and so on

One of the key issues surrounding quality is whether or not the quality, however defined, is understood by all the relevant parties concerned, i.e.

- *The organisation enabling the service provision*

- *The organisation providing the service (may be the same as the above)*

- *The employees delivering the service*

- *The consumers of the service*

The understanding of the quality definition needs to be consistent amongst all the above parties to ensure that "quality" means the same thing for everyone. One way to ensure this happens is to have effective internal and external communication systems.

The relationships and influences that help determine the quality definition are represented diagrammatically as follows:

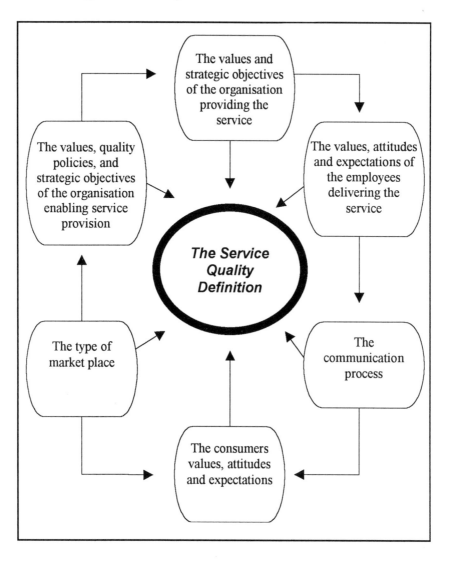

An example of how all the parties should interact with respect to defining quality is shown as follows:

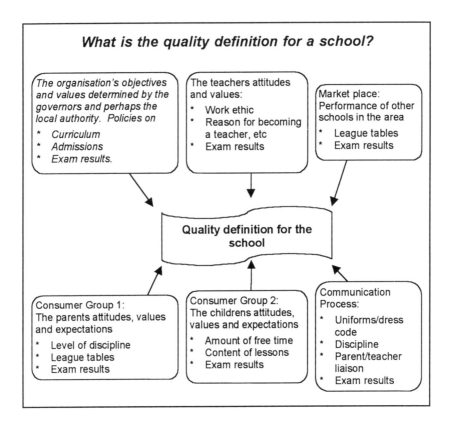

All perspectives in the above example show that exam results need to be part of the quality definition for this particular school.

Establishing a Quality Framework

In order to establish a quality environment, the organisation ideally needs to have a framework within which quality can be developed and maintained. As with most frameworks, quality should begin at the top of the organisation and be reflected in the overall goals and objectives.

The framework also needs to include:

- ❖ Quality policies and procedures

- ❖ Methods of gaining customer/user feedback

- ❖ Methods of gaining employee feedback

- ❖ Methods of gaining market information on quality

- ❖ A process for establishing quality definitions and standards

- ❖ A process for communication between all parties, both internal and external

- ❖ Methods for implementing, measuring, monitoring and evaluating the quality of service

- ❖ A process for continuous improvements

When the quality framework is in place, it should be linked in a coordinated way to produce a cycle for continuous quality development.

The cycle for continuous quality development can be represented by the following diagram.

Cycle for continuous quality development

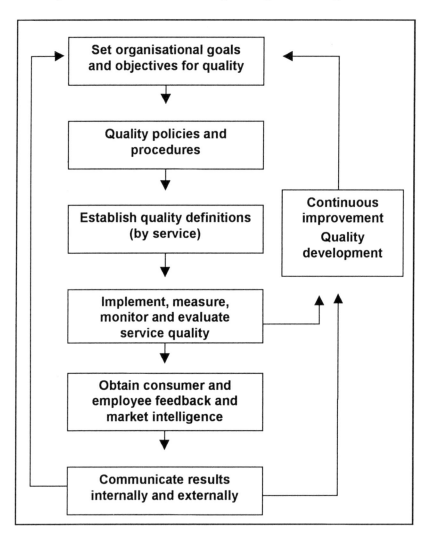

SUMMARY

✧ Quality can be useful in helping public sector organisations to achieve value for money, in setting quality thresholds for service provision and creating an image

✧ Defining quality is difficult therefore a quality definition needs to be developed for individual services and products

✧ There are a number of factors involved in defining quality, including the values of the organisation, it's customers and employees

✧ The market place may be helpful in determining acceptable quality levels

✧ A quality framework helps the organisation to define quality and achieve continuous improvement

✧ The quality framework should include a number of factors such as quality policies and procedures, methods of gaining customer feedback, methods of gaining employee feedback and methods of gaining market information with respect to quality

Exercise 1

Values and Objectives
~ Impact on Quality ~

For the following examples, set out what you consider to be:

a) The most important values

b) The key strategic objectives

c) The impact on quality

A person who purchases *a Rolls Royce*	*A person who purchases* *a Mini*
VALUES:	*VALUES:*
OBJECTIVES:	*OBJECTIVES:*
IMPACT ON QUALITY:	*IMPACT ON QUALITY:*

Suggested solutions to this exercise can be found on page 117.

Exercise 2

Service Quality Definitions

1. Identify below, the five most influential values to a local authority and the five most important values to a private business. What impact do these have on the way quality would be defined for the delivery of a school bus service?

Public Sector Values

1) ....

2) ....

3) ....

4) ....

5) ....

Quality Definition for School Bus Service

Private Sector Values

1) ....

2) ....

3) ....

4) ....

5) ....

Quality Definition for School Bus Service

Suggested solutions to this exercise can be found on page 118

Exercise 3

Service Quality Definitions

Consider one or more of your services, and using the following categories, identify with respect to each category, the factors which are taken into account when establishing service quality.

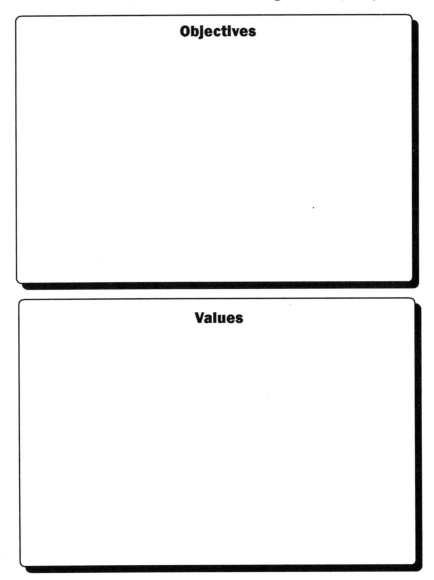

Objectives

Values

Consumer Attitudes and Expectations

Employee Attitudes and Expectations

Market Place

Communication Methods

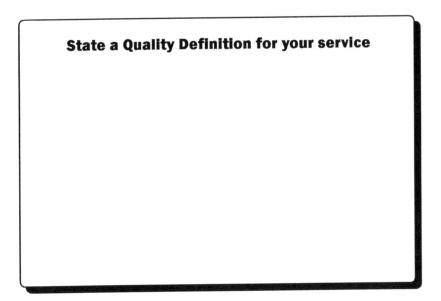

State a Quality Definition for your service

Chapter 3

SETTING QUALITY STANDARDS

Purpose of Quality Standards

Having developed a quality definition, quality standards are then used to set out tangible benchmarks against which service delivery can be measured. For any given product or service this is a particularly important way of letting the public know what is meant by "quality". Within the public sector, quality standards are increasingly being published.

Quality standards should provide the following:

❖ A clear statement of what the consumer can expect from the service

❖ A clear statement of how employees are expected to perform with respect to service delivery

❖ A benchmark for monitoring the service and the extent to which quality standards are being met

❖ A basis for distinguishing the quality of your service from those of other providers

❖ A basis for evaluating services and assessing value for money

- ❖ A basis for the preparation of service specifications to be adhered to by internal and external service providers
- ❖ A basis for allocating resources

Types of Quality Standards

Quality standards are usually developed at two levels:

Tangible:	Based on a service specification where the service is broken down into detailed processes and functions which can be documented with specific and tangible outcomes.
Intangible:	Based on relationship/interaction between provider and consumer, e.g. How helpful were staff? Was information given in a way that could be understood? etc.

Tangible standards, such as response times, are easier to set than the intangible ones such as helpfulness and attitude.

Examples of quality standards given by a local authority housing department are shown in the following table.

Type of Service Activity	Quality Standard	Tangible	Intangible
New estate action bids	Ensure full tenant involvement and satisfaction		✓
Provide smoke alarms	To British Standards	✓	
Establish a housing advice shop	Provide impartial advice and information		✓
Major structural repairs to defective dwellings	To comply with current building regulations	✓	
Central repairs reporting	Respond to caller within 15 seconds	✓	
Void property repairs	To prepare properties for letting to a standard that achieves a letting on a first viewing	✓	

Some organisations identify different achievement levels within a quality standard allowing for:

The Ideal
(standards are fully met i.e. zero defect)

The Attainable
(standards are met within an acceptable range, e.g. 95% of the time)

The Minimum
(below which is an unacceptable level of quality; for many organisations this is usually the current level of service quality)

All organisations should be striving towards the ideal which means there is always scope for improvement. (See cycle for continuous quality development, page 12).

In the private sector, standards are often underwritten with generous promises, e.g.

> *"30 days free trial and if not totally satisfied with the product your money back"*

> *"If we are more than 20 minutes late with your pizza delivery you don't have to pay"*

Some services, such as those delivered by certain professions, have standards set out in guidelines and ethical codes. These standards are monitored by the relevant professional bodies.

Other standards are enforceable because they are underwritten by legislation, and if these standards are not met the consumer may, in some instances, sue for compensation.

An example of how standards should be defined was set out in the government's white Paper on the Citizen's Charter (HSMO 1991) "The citizen must be told what service standards are and be able to act where service is unacceptable".

> *"Explicit standards, published and prominently displayed at the point of delivery. These standards should invariably include courtesy and helpfulness from staff, accuracy in accordance with statutory entitlements, and a commitment to prompt action, which might be expressed in terms of a target response or waiting time. If targets are to be stretched, it may not be possible to guarantee them in every case; minimum, as well as average, standards may be necessary. There should be a clear presumption that standards will be progressively improved as services become more efficient."*

Developing Standards for Public Sector Services

There is an increasing demand for public sector services to be of "high quality", and in some areas the public sector has to shake off the image of "poor quality". Once quality has been defined, the organisation has to translate it into documented standards that can be measured and monitored.

It may be very difficult to establish standards for certain types of public sector service. For example:

❖ Services for which it is difficult to define quality in the first instance, e.g. prevention type services

❖ Services were the concept of quality differs greatly between the service provider and consumer, e.g. enforcement type services

❖ Services where quality is totally subjective, e.g. caring type services

If a structured approach is taken to developing standards some of these difficulties can be overcome.

The approach to be taken is to break down the service into its composite stages as follows:

❖ Input

❖ Process

❖ Output

❖ Outcome

At each of the above stages, there will be varying degrees of interaction between the service provider, the employees, and the recipients of the service. It is through this interaction that quality standards can be developed at each stage. Depending on the nature of the service, developing standards will prove more difficult at some stages than at others. By taking this approach, all aspects of the service will be taken into account, and not just those areas where standards are easy to develop.

Input, process, output and outcome standards are discussed further below.

Input Standards

These relate to those factors required to deliver the service. Inputs include:

- *Staffing resources*
- *Physical resources*
- *Financial resources*
- *Customer enquiries*

Quality standards can be developed around each of these, for example:

Input	Standards
Staff	Qualifications, experience, attitude, service knowledge, etc.
Facilities	Accessibility, fitness for purpose, sufficiency, etc.
Finance	Level, accessibility, variability, etc.
Enquiries	Accuracy, completeness, clarity, relevance, etc.

An example of possible input standards for a school is given as follows:

Teachers: *Set standards with respect to their qualifications and experience in teaching each subject*

Pupils: *Set standards with respect to how pupils are allocated to the school and classes within the school. (This does not necessarily mean adopting controversial methods of assessment resulting in selection based purely on academic ability)*

School environment: *Set standards with respect to school buildings, playing areas, class sizes, school meals, and so on*

Finances: *Set standards with respect to budgets, charges, collection, administration, and so on*

Process Standards

The process aspect of a service is "how" it is delivered. For some services the process is clearly documented and broken down into a number of steps, each of which can be standardised, monitored and controlled. Other services are very individual in nature and hence the process is different in every case, although there may be a commonality of approach to service delivery.

The starting point for setting standards with regard to the process of service delivery is to identify the common features of the service.

For example, an advice centre will give different advice depending on the circumstances of each case, however there may be a common way to conduct a meeting, keep records, validate advice given, and so on. Quality standards can be set around all of these areas. This still does not address the point as to whether the advice given was "quality advice", i.e. in line with the quality definition for the service. The quality of the advice may be very subjective and the output from the service may assist in determining the quality of the advice. However, setting standards for the advice may be achieved by asking advice givers to identify when they consider they have done a good job and set standards around those attributes.

The quality of the process will be affected by the quality of the original input, hence the importance of ensuring that the input meets certain quality standards.

Output Standards

Unlike a product, the output from a service is not always tangible, and hence the standards for output may be difficult to devise. Output standards should be developed around the following areas.

Output	Standards
Tangible evidence, e.g. a report, a placement, a decision, a penalty, etc.	Content, timing, accessibility, responsiveness, staff attitudes and behaviour, etc.
Consumer satisfaction	Consumer feedback, levels of satisfaction, levels of complaints, methods of communication, etc.
Cure, solution, etc.	Timing, comparative results, safety, costs, etc.

The following example considers how quality standards may be developed for outputs:

One of the outputs from the fire service is extinguishing a fire. This would be considered to be a cure/solution output. The quality standards that could be developed for this would include the speed with which the fire was extinguished; the level of safety adopted; and the cost. Other standards such as customer satisfaction levels would also apply, but may not be as important to the overall quality definition, i.e. safety and speed may take priority.

Outcome Standards

The eventual outcome from a service is often unknown and it may require a great deal of resources to establish what the outcome actually is. These resources may not always be available to the public sector, however, this does not mean that quality standards cannot be set with respect to outcomes. In many cases, standards are most likely to be based on "expected" outcomes as opposed to "actual" outcomes. These expected outcomes may be based on research and may be general, as opposed to specific, for the individual service in question.

Whilst outputs can lead to a wide range of possible outcomes, in some cases outcomes and outputs may be the same. Some of the more common outcomes can be generalised into the following categories:

Outcome	Standards
Prevention	Reduction in incidents (crime, sickness, accidents, etc.)
Quality of life	Health, education, wealth, employment, social behaviour, etc.
Environment	Cleanliness, health, safety, conservation, image, etc.
Consumer satisfaction	Long term shift in attitudes, changes in consumer behaviour, consumer education, etc.

For example, when social services make a decision to place a child in foster care the expected outcome will be to enhance the quality of life for the child. Standards can be set as to the incremental benefits that should be gained in respect to some of the quality of life benchmarks.

It is clear from the above that there is a considerable amount of work required if appropriate standards are to be developed for all services at all levels, and it will take time.

The quality definition is fundamental to the process of setting standards and an organisation may have to go back to this stage before being able to develop a range of standards that are relevant and meaningful.

SUMMARY

✧ Quality standards provide a benchmark for measuring the quality of service provision

✧ Quality standards should be published so that consumers and staff know what they are

✧ Quality standards may be tangible and intangible. Tangible ones are easier to set

✧ Services should be broken down to reflect input, process and output requirements and expected outcomes. Standards should be set in all areas

✧ Some services may be input driven, particularly where outputs and outcomes are difficult to define

✧ The quality definition is fundamental to developing appropriate quality standards

Exercise 4

Quality Standards

Insert your public sector definition for the School Bus Service from Exercise 2, then set a number of tangible and intangible quality standards that you would be prepared to put on show to the general public.

QUALITY DEFINITION

QUALITY STANDARDS

Tangible

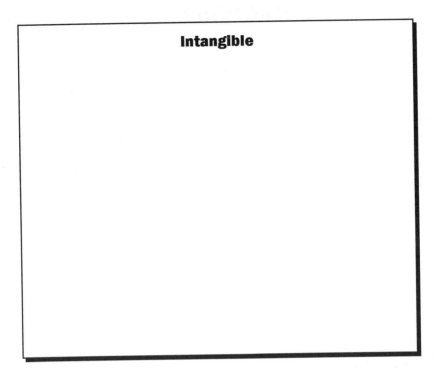

Intangible

Suggested solutions to this exercise can be found on page 119.

Exercise 5

Quality Standards

P<small>ART</small> (A)

List the current quality standards that have been developed for your service area and analyse them in the following way. (If you have none, go on to part B).

Standard	Tangible	Intangible	Input	Process	Output	Outcome
e.g. *we respond to an enquiry within 5 working days of receipt*	☑	☐	☐	☑	☑	☐
	☐	☐	☐	☐	☐	☐
	☐	☐	☐	☐	☐	☐
	☐	☐	☐	☐	☐	☐
	☐	☐	☐	☐	☐	☐
	☐	☐	☐	☐	☐	☐
	☐	☐	☐	☑	☐	☐

(Answers will vary according to the nature and the quality definition of your service)

Part (B)

Where there are gaps in the current range of standards, consider the new standards that need to be put in place; e.g. there may be output standards but no input ones or vice versa.

Standard	Tangible	Intangible	Input	Process	Output	Outcome
	☐	☐	☐	☐	☐	☐
	☐	☐	☐	☐	☐	☐
	☐	☐	☐	☐	☐	☐
	☐	☐	☐	☐	☐	☐
	☐	☐	☐	☐	☐	☐
	☐	☐	☐	☐	☐	☐
	☐	☐	☐	☐	☐	☐

PART (C)

For the new standards identified in part B, list the potential difficulties in setting and implementing them and how you consider those difficulties may be overcome.

Difficulties in Setting the Standards	Possible Solutions

Chapter 4

MEASURING AND MONITORING QUALITY

Performance Indicators

Having established quality standards for a service, it is in the interest of the organisation, staff and consumers to identify how actual service delivery measures up to those standards. To achieve this, the organisation/service provider should identify the most appropriate indicators of quality given the standards that have been set. These performance indicators can then be used as part of the performance measurement process. It is only with consistent measurement over time that organisations can make a judgement as to the level of actual quality being achieved.

In chapter 3 quality standards were broken down into two main categories, tangible and intangible. Performance indicators need to be developed for both types of standard so as to provide tangible evidence of measurement. When performance indicators have been developed they can be used as a basis for setting performance targets. These targets may allow for some element of non-performance, particularly for services where it may not be possible to achieve 100% success, 100% of the time.

A wide range of suitable performance indicators can be developed for some services, but a practical approach needs to be taken to identify the indicators that are most important with respect to the desired level of quality. This selection can be achieved by obtaining a consensus between provider and consumer as to what aspects of the service are the most important when determining the quality definition.

Performance indicators tend to fall into two categories:

QUANTITATIVE   *QUALITATIVE*

Most services will attract both types of indicator, however, it is far easier to measure quantitative indicators rather than qualitative ones.

In order to assist in identifying the type of performance indicators that are relevant for a particular service, one needs to ask the following questions:

A re any of the inputs critical to the service quality standard?

A re there any processes critical to the service quality standard?

W hat are the outputs that reflect the quality standards?

W hat outcome is expected from the service?

I s there scope to improve the service quality and redefine the standard?

An example is given as follows:

Service:	*Meals on wheels*
Quality Definition:	*To provide a caring delivery service of tasty, nutritious hot meals, to all eligible clients between 12.00pm and 1.00pm daily*
Extract from published Quality Standards:	<ul><li>*Meals will be delivered within 10 minutes of the agreed time*</li><li>*Meals will be varied each day with high nutritional value and be hot on arrival at client's premises*</li><li>*Staff will be courteous and helpful at all times*</li></ul>

Performance Indicators	*Quantitative*	*Qualitative*
Time of delivery to client	✓	
Range of menus offered each day	✓	✓
Temperature of meals on arrival	✓	
Number of meals provided each day	✓	
Nutritional value of ingredients	✓	✓
Method of food preparation	✓	✓
Staff qualifications	✓	✓
Method of delivery	✓	✓
Level of staff training	✓	✓
Friendliness of staff		✓
Time spent at the client's premises	✓	✓
Customer satisfaction	✓	✓

It should be noted that many of the performance indicators identified in the example can be both quantitative and qualitative.

Having identified the indicators of performance with respect to the quality standards, the next stage is to develop sensible methods of measuring the indicators which are not too time consuming or bureaucratic.

Measuring Performance

In the same way that indicators have been identified as quantitative and qualitative, so can the way in which those indicators are measured. There may be several different ways of measuring the same indicator. The important factor to remember is that measurement should be practical and should not result in the need for lots of additional resources, otherwise this becomes an additional cost of quality.

Using the performance indicators identified in the previous meals on wheels example, we can identify the following appropriate quantitative and qualitative performance measures

Performance Indicator	Performance Measure (Quantitative)	Performance Measure (Qualitative)
Time of delivery to client	Log of arrival time at each client	
Range of menus offered each day	Number of different menus offered each day	Content of each menu offered
Temperature of meals on arrival	Temperature readings on arrival at clients premises Temperature of containers used by provider	

Performance Indicator	Performance Measure (Quantitative)	Performance Measure (Qualitative)
Number of meals provided each day	Count of number of meals packaged for delivery Count of number of meals delivered	
Nutritional value of ingredients	Percentage of menu that includes "fresh" produce	Inspection of site during preparation and observation of "fresh" produce use
Method of food production	Audit of quality system in place for food production logging number of exceptions to the system	Observation of methods used and general assessment of key indicators such as cleanliness, health and safety, etc.
Qualifications/ experience of staff	CVs of staff engaged in the service	Observing staff ability to perform certain functions
Method of delivery	Audit of delivery system and logging number of exceptions	Inspection of modes of transport used during delivery and general assessment of key indicators such as fitness for purpose, presentation of vehicle, etc.
Level of staff training	Detailed staff training records identifying number of days per person per annum undertaken	Details of range and content of training courses undertaken
Friendliness of staff		Client opinions gained from client surveys Staff opinions gained from staff surveys Observation and general assessment of staff on site
Time spent at the client's premises	Log of arrival time and departure time from each client	Client opinion of customer care gained from client surveys
Customer satisfaction	Customer satisfaction survey results for tangible indicators, e.g. food was hot	Customer satisfaction survey for intangible indicators such as staff were helpful, caring, etc.

For each of these measures, targets should be set which act as a benchmark, for example:

- ❖ Specify number of menu choices that should be on offer
- ❖ Specify number of meals that should be produced daily
- ❖ Specify the temperature range of the food
- ❖ Specify the level of exceptions allowed when quality systems audited
- ❖ Specify the level of customer satisfaction expected

The purpose of undertaking measurement is to ensure that targets for performance are being met and the quality standards are being maintained. Where organisations fail to meet the targets, reasons for failure should be investigated. Depending on the reasons for failing to meet standards, it may be necessary to redefine the quality standard to take account of changed conditions, unforeseen problems, and so on.

Performance measurement is therefore important for the following reasons, it:

- ❖ Identifies whether or not quality standards are being met
- ❖ Identifies changes that need to be made to the service in order to meet quality standards (where possible)
- ❖ Identifies whether or not quality standards need to be revised (upwards or downwards)

❖ Provides a tangible method of identifying under performance, which in the case of a client/contractor relationship, may be the basis for penalties

❖ Provides the public with information on the standard of service being provided

Monitoring Techniques

In order to monitor quality standards, efficient and effective data collection systems need to be in place. This data should give a measure of performance which will indicate whether or not performance targets have been met. Performance monitoring ought to be undertaken on a regular basis.

If the organisation has a philosophy of continuous improvement, the results of monitoring should feed into service developments and new quality standards. There are many public sector organisations which consider that although continuous improvement is great in theory, in practice the real focus is to continuously achieve more for less. Even in these instances, performance monitoring will still highlight the impact of reducing resources and perhaps identify ways in which standards can be maintained and targets met within a climate of cuts and savings.

Performance can be monitored at a number of levels within any organisation:

Corporate Level

Monitoring	Method
Monitoring the achievement of strategic objectives as set out in the business plan, comparing what is actually happening with what is set out in the plan, and identifying why variances have occurred.	• Regular business plan review meetings • Regular revision of business plan and communication of reviews and revisions • Regular assessment of values and quality policy

Operational Level

Monitoring	Method
Monitoring the delivery of services, ensuring that the standards are being maintained by collecting data and measuring actual performance against the standard	• Analysing data collected from the measurement of performance indicators • Identifying areas where performance is not meeting set standards • Identifying areas for improvement and setting out appropriate action plans • Undertaking regular system audits to ensure information is accurate and complete

Individual Level

Monitoring	Method
Monitoring individual performance against planned targets	• Setting targets at appraisal meetings • Reviewing targets at regular management meetings • Identifying areas where targets are not being met, and dealing with the reasons for non-performance • Setting individual action plans

In order to assist in performance monitoring, clear goals, objectives and targets should be set and backed up with action plans which identify what needs to be done, by whom, and by when.

Responsibility for performance monitoring is held at all levels within the organisation:

Directors ~ **Corporate level**

Managers ~ **Operational level, services and resource management**

All staff ~ **Individual level, self monitoring, attitude, work ethic, etc.**

The achievement and monitoring of quality standards is dependent on how well standards are initially set, and the quality systems in place that allow sufficient and appropriate data to be collected so as to measure performance. This means that standards need to be constantly reviewed, and performance measures should become increasingly sophisticated such that the organisation, the management and all staff adopt the values of a quality culture.

SUMMARY

◇ Having set quality standards, it is in the interest of the organisation, staff and consumers to measure how the actual service delivery measures up to those standards

◇ Performance indicators need to be developed for tangible and intangible standards

◇ When performance indicators have been developed they can be used as a basis for setting performance targets

◇ Performance indicators tend to fall into two categories: quantitative and qualitative

◇ Most services will attract both quantitative and qualitative indicators, however, it is far easier to measure quantitative indicators than qualitative ones

◇ The purpose of undertaking measurement is to ensure that performance targets are being met and therefore the quality standard is being maintained

◇ Where organisations fail to meet the targets, reasons for failure should be investigated

◇ Depending on the reasons for failing to meet standards, it may be necessary to redefine the quality standard to take account of changes in conditions, unforeseen problems, and so on

◇ In order to monitor quality standards successfully, there needs to be an efficient and effective data collection system

◇ In order to assist in the monitoring of performance, clear goals, objectives and targets need to be set and backed up with actions plans which identify what needs to be done, by whom, and by when

◇ Responsibility for performance monitoring is held at all levels within the organisation

◇ The achievement and monitoring of quality standards is dependent on how well standards are initially set

◇ Standards need to be constantly reviewed, and performance measures need to become increasingly sophisticated, such that the organisation, the management and all staff adopt the values of a quality culture

Exercise 6

Performance Indicators

For each standard identified in Exercise 4, list at least two performance indicators (think about how they might be measured).

Standard	Performance Indicators

Standard	Performance Indicators

Suggested solutions to this exercise can be found on page 120.

Exercise 7

Measuring Performance

Given the scenarios set out on pages 52 and 53, answer the following for each case:

a)   Is this a quality service?

Case 1

Case 2

Case 3

b) What type of performance measurement would you undertake?

Case 1

Case 2

Case 3

c) How could the service be improved?

Case 1

Case 2

Case 3

Suggested solutions to this exercise can be found on page 122.

Case 1

The finance department produces financial control reports on a monthly basis which give managers information about the budget and actual spending in their departments. One of their quality standards is that these reports should be delivered within two weeks of the month end, and another is that they will process corrections within one month. On the whole, they have managed to achieve both of these quality standards. However, managers are concerned that the information is usually incorrect and out of date and therefore of little use, many managers often only file the reports. Some managers are considering setting up their own reports in order to obtain better information.

Case 2

The street cleansing service is supposed to sweep every footpath once per week and empty bins on those footpaths once per week as per the specification in their contract. Their performance standard is that all rubbish and debris is removed from the footpath and all rubbish is removed from the bins and surrounding area after they have been emptied and swept. The DSO performs it's duty as per the specification.

Case 3

The front of house reception has recently undergone major restructuring with a view to introducing a quality service. The authority has described a quality reception service as "A reception where all people are treated with dignity and respect in a prompt and efficient manner." The quality standards for reception have been stated and displayed as follows:

◆ *All enquiries at the front desk will be responded to within five minutes*

◆ *No one will be kept waiting in reception for more than ten minutes without being referred on to the appropriate service, e.g. cashiers, planning, etc.*

◆ *Receptionists will give out accurate information to all enquiries and provide practical assistance wherever possible*

◆ *Receptionists will maintain several information systems including visitors books, databases, enquiry logs, distribution of information records and service utilization records*

There are four receptionists who are supposed to work together as a team on a shift basis such that two people are present at all times. One of the receptionists has raised several issues with the manager:

◆ *Not all receptionists can use the computer, therefore, most of the inputting is left to one person, whilst the others are not always using the computer to obtain the most up to date information*

◆ *Although waiting times have been adhered to, quite often, the departments who are supposed to deal with the enquirer do not respond promptly, so people are ushered into interview rooms (not waiting in reception) to wait for quite a long time*

◆ *Some receptionists are not very helpful and redirect enquiries that they could have dealt with immediately with the available information at the reception desk*

The manager responsible for reception feels that things are going well as there have not been any complaints as yet (there used to be at least 3 per week) and the management information systems seem to be kept up to date and identify that enquiries are being dealt with in a proper manner.

Exercise 8

Measuring Performance

Given the quality standards for your own service, set out the ways in which you currently measure performance against the standard. Think about other ways in which performance measurement and monitoring could be undertaken.

Type of Service:			
Service Standard	Performance Indicators	Measurement Methods	New Ways of Measurement

Chapter 5

QUALITY MANAGEMENT

Total Quality Management

To operate an effective quality management process, the whole organisation has to be involved in total quality management. This requires effective quality systems which covers the whole range of activities from the inputs to the outcomes.

Total quality management needs to operate at a number of levels as shown below.

Strategic Level

Focus on:

- ■ *Achieving long term objectives*
- ■ *Establishing the overarching mission to which everyone works*
- ■ *Developing the corporate image*
- ■ *Survival of the organisation*

Owned by senior management

Operational Level

Focus on:

- Standard processes and procedures
- Team working
- Increasing productivity
- Reducing waste and errors
- Achieving consistency

Owned by managers and the workforce

Customer Level

Focus on:

- Meeting customer requirements
- Establishing customer perceptions
- Anticipating future customer needs
- Changing to meet external demands
- Achieving customer satisfaction

Owned by marketing departments and some front-line staff

Development Level

Focus on:

- Staff development
- Staff training
- Staff participation
- Individual responsibility
- Individual performance

Owned by personnel departments and some managers

In order to develop a truly quality organisation, ideally all members of the organisation should feel part of and own all levels of total quality management. To achieve this, the following types of under pinning processes should be in place:

❖ Business planning cycles

❖ Performance management systems

❖ Appraisal systems

❖ Quality circles

❖ Codes of practice

❖ Quality manuals

❖ Consumer liaison

These points are discussed further in the following paragraphs.

Business Planning Cycles

Quality is dependent upon the organisational objectives and these are developed as part of the business planning process. Therefore, business planning is a fundamental underpinning quality system which is essential if the organisation is to become truly quality orientated. The business plan will have objectives around products, services, marketing and so on, all of which will have a quality dimension. The business plan will identify targets and strategies which will enable objectives to be achieved.

Business plans should be developed on a regular basis as part of a routine, and where possible, all parts of the organisation should be involved. The business planning cycle is an ongoing process which enables continual review and evaluation of objectives, taking account of internal and external factors.

Performance Management Systems

Some organisations incorporate performance management as part of their overall appraisal system. The concept of performance management advocates that all staff have specific targets to work towards and are managed in a way which encourages them to be innovative. In so doing, staff are not only encouraged to meet their targets, but to exceed them. Performance management is often linked to a reward system which allows managers to give credit to those staff who have performed successfully. Quality should be built into the targets that are given to staff and hence it should be measured as part of the overall measurement of staff performance. In order for a performance management system to play an effective role in establishing a quality organisation, it has to be implemented at all levels and monitored on a regular basis; an annual review is insufficient to ensure that staff are implementing their duties to the required quality standards.

Appraisal Systems

The appraisal system is fundamental to the quality organisation and most of the recognised quality kite marks expect organisations to have an effective appraisal system in place. It is important that the appraisal system used has the following features:

- It links the individual's targets to the organisations' objectives

- It involves interaction between the appraiser and appraisee

- The appraiser is trained on how to conduct an appraisal

- There is consistency across the organisation as to how the appraisal is undertaken and the results used

- Appraisals happen at least once per year

- The appraisal covers all aspects of the individual's work including less tangible areas such as attitudes

- The appraisee understands how he/she is performing and what needs to be done in the case of under performance

- The appraisal sets targets for future periods

- The appraisal identifies future training needs which are fed into the training plans for the individual and the organisation

In addition to the above, some appraisals have scoring systems which may link into reward systems or be used as a basis for recommending promotions.

The appraisal can be a powerful tool with respect to ensuring that staff understand and implement the quality standards within the organisation.

Quality Circles

A quality circle is a form of working group whereby a number of staff come together in order to improve the quality of their product or service. This is one of a variety of techniques that involves the workforce in maintaining and developing quality within the organisation, and hence can be a useful tool for maintaining a quality organisation.

The quality circle will include a group of staff led by a supervisor, not too large (up to 10) who are performing the same or similar work.

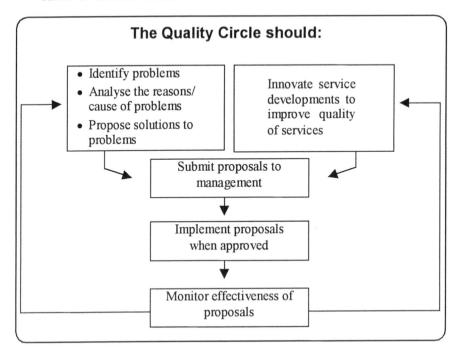

Ultimately the quality circle should become sufficiently trusted within an organisation such that the management decision making function can be devolved to lower levels. This will allow the process to move more quickly by eliminating unnecessary bureaucracy. Research has shown that quality circles only tend to work in organisations that are quality centred and where many of the other underpinning quality processes are in place.

Codes of Practice

These codes give staff guidance as to how to deliver services, including aspects which are linked to quality. The codes may be internal or provided by external bodies with a monitoring role (particularly true of professions). A quality organisation will ensure that all such codes are strictly enforced. Breaches of the code may result in staff being disciplined and, depending on the type of breach, losing their professional standing.

Quality Manuals

These are usually internally developed by the organisation and set down the quality standard for each aspect of the service. Ideally the manual will break down the service into its component parts and provide staff with a clear understanding of how the service should be delivered, and their role in ensuring a quality service is produced. Some quality manuals are so large they are not user friendly. Ideally the quality manual should be an accessible tool for all staff, enabling them to achieve the correct quality levels for all aspects of the service. In order to develop a successful quality manual, the following issues should be considered:

- The quality principles underlying the organisation and its approach to service delivery

- Development of a clear service specification, i.e. services should be clearly defined along with quantitative and qualitative quality standards

- Breaking the service down into its component elements, stages, etc.

- Identifying the input, process, output, and outcome of each stage

- The quality performance indicators that will be measured and monitored in order to ensure the quality standards are achieved

- How the service can be audited to ensure that the procedures set out in the manual are being adhered to

- Staff involvement staff in all aspects of the above

Quality manuals benefit from the use of flow charts which are simple to understand and user friendly. Developing flow charts often assist staff to think about exactly how the service is delivered and can often result in changes and enhancements being made to the service which then lead to quality improvements.

Consumer Liaison

As public sector organisations are typically service oriented, it is important that they have an effective method of communicating with service users/consumers. This is the group which often determines acceptable quality standards. A quality organisation should put in place a consumer liaison process which allows for feedback on existing services and suggestions for potential new service developments. This can be achieved by implementing some of the following:

- Frequent consumer surveys

- Focus groups

- Consumer consultation on change/developments

- Consumer participation (e.g. representation on boards of management, committees, working parties, and so on)

- Suggestion boxes

- Feedback sheets

- Public meetings

- Open days

- Newsletters

- Complaints procedures

Quality Audits

The audit is a fundamental part of quality control and therefore an essential process for a quality organisation. The audit of quality systems highlight the extent and frequency with which quality standards are being met; for example, 90% of the service meets the standard 85% of the time.

Where the service has undergone the process of establishing a quality definition, quality standards, performance indicators, measurement processes and continual monitoring, the quality audit should be relatively straightforward.

It is common for quality audits to be undertaken internally with an officer having responsibility for auditing the systems. This may be a specialist post, or there may be a specialist department responsible for quality. Another approach is to make responsibility for quality audits part of the managers overall responsibilities. Ideally those responsible for quality audits should:

❖ Have a clear understanding of what the organisation wishes to achieve from the audits performed

❖ Be independent of the service being delivered (i.e. not part of the delivery team)

❖ Have no vested interest in the outcome of the audit

❖ Have relevant service knowledge (i.e. knows what to look out for)

❖ Have sufficient standing in the organisation to get recommendations implemented

These criteria favour the independent auditor as opposed to the manger. However, there are benefits in having someone close to the service, such as the manager, undertaking regular audits. These include:

❖ Detailed service knowledge

❖ Understanding the problems that may be the cause of poor performance and non-achievement of standards

❖ Speed of corrective action (no need to wait for an external report)

❖ Ownership of the quality system

❖ Responsibility and accountability for meeting quality standards

Audits are often seen as intrusive with someone "checking up" on staff to ensure that they are performing their jobs properly. Further, they are typically associated with the monitoring of the organisation's finances and financial systems, often with the emphasis on detecting fraud. Auditors are therefore frequently viewed with suspicion by other staff in the organisation.

This should not be the case, especially with respect to the audit of quality systems. The purpose of the audit should be fully explained and seek to:

- ❖ Identify what standards are being achieved and how often

- ❖ Identify areas where quality standards are falling short of the acceptable levels

- ❖ Ensure the measurement and monitoring processes are being implemented

- ❖ Suggest new ways to measure and monitor quality where the existing ones are proving inadequate

- ❖ Provide recommendations for improvements to all aspects of service delivery including the quality of input, process, output and outcome.

- ❖ Produce a written report which can be reviewed, and progress monitored at subsequent audits

The audit therefore benefits the whole organisation.

In some cases auditors that are external to the organisation are engaged to audit quality systems. These may be quality consultants, or professional bodies which monitor standards for their professional membership. Where an organisation has achieved a quality kite mark of some kind such as ISO 9000, the awarding body undertakes a regular assessment, similar to an audit, to ensure that the organisation continues to meet the standards that have been set.

SUMMARY

✧ Total quality management needs to operate at the following levels:

- ◆ Strategic
- ◆ Operational
- ◆ Customer
- ◆ Development

✧ Ideally all members of the organisation should feel part of, and own, all levels of total quality management

✧ In order to develop and maintain a quality organisation, there needs to be underpinning processes such as business planning cycles, performance management systems, appraisal systems, quality circles, codes of practice, quality manuals and consumer liaison processes

✧ In order for a performance management system to play an effective role in establishing a quality organisation, it has to be implemented at all levels and monitored on a regular basis

✧ Quality systems need to be regularly audited

✧ Audits can be undertaken by internal or external experts, ideally they should be totally independent of the service

Exercise 9

Total Quality Management in Practice

A Prison Service provider (APS) recently took management of a prison which had the following problems:

⇨ *Very poor staff relations*

⇨ *A reputation for regular riots*

⇨ *Poor working conditions*

⇨ *Dull and dirty common areas*

⇨ *Provision of a very limited range of activities (partly due to lack of appropriate staffing)*

⇨ *Poor standards of catering (meals low on variety and nutrition)*

⇨ *Very bad image with local residents and prison visitors*

The new contract manager decided that the best way forward would be to look at the whole organisation and implement a total quality management approach to all aspects of prison life.

The time scale for implementation was one year, as after this time APS would have its first performance assessment. The key performance targets included:

⇨ *Decrease in staff turnover*

⇨ *Reduction in number of riots*

⇨ *Reduction in number of complaints*

⇨ *Refurbishment of common areas*

⇨ *Increased number of activities*

APS won the tender based on a 10% saving on historical costs and therefore performance targets have to be achieved within a lower budget than had previously been spent on the prison, i.e. any new changes will have to be very low cost in order to stay within budget.

The manager needs to develop a list of actions setting out all the things she wishes to do in order to start developing a total quality management system.

> *Given the above, identify a list of actions covering all aspects of the organisation which you consider the manager should undertake.*

1 _____

2 _____

3 _____

4 _____

5 _____

6 _____

7 _____

8 _____

9 _____

10 _____

Suggested solutions to this exercise can be found on page 124.

Exercise 10

TQM Systems

Describe how you would implement TQM in your area of service

List the implementation stages:

_____

_____

_____

_____

_____

_____

_____

_____

What problems may you encounter in trying to operate a TQM system?

Chapter 6

INVESTING IN QUALITY

Cost of Quality

It is often assumed that increasing service quality requires an increase in cost. Hence, many people associate a more expensive service with higher quality. These two assumptions are in many cases untrue. The relationship between quality and cost can be wide and varied depending on the nature of the service or product being delivered.

The following diagrams illustrate a number of relationships between cost and quality

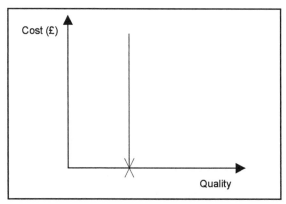

Same quality regardless of cost

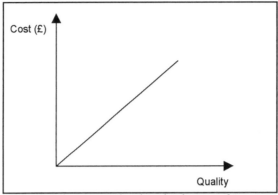

Higher costs lead to higher quality

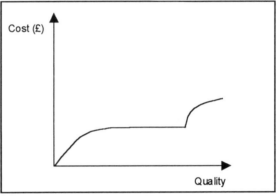

Quality increases initially with cost until a certain point whereby quality continues to increase without additional cost. After a while further quality improvements require further investment. This is the most typical profile

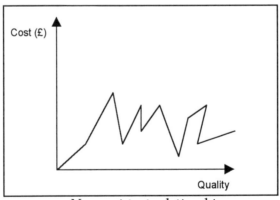

No consistent relationship between quality and cost

In order to determine the quality/cost relationship for a service, the organisation needs to establish its definition of "Quality" and of "Cost". Defining quality has been discussed in chapter 2.

The cost of quality for a service should take into account the following:

❖ What key factors enhance service quality?

❖ What inputs are required to implement those factors?

❖ Do the inputs represent a direct additional cost, if so, how much?

❖ What are the differences in outputs and outcomes as a result of the enhancement to quality and can these be measured in tangible terms?

When assessing the cost of quality it is necessary to take account of all costs such as:

❖ Those costs directly attributable to quality enhancement, e.g. the cost of an additional member of staff providing additional service, the cost of training, the cost of refurbishment, and so on

❖ Those costs indirectly resulting from increasing the level of quality, e.g. increased service demand

An example of how the cost and quality relationship can be assessed is given as follows:

A local authority had very poor satisfaction ratings for its advice centre and decided to increase the quality of service. The quality definition for the service being:

> **"a fast response to the public's enquiries giving accurate and complete information which meets their requirements"**

The quality improvements would include:

Quality Improvement	*Cost (£)*
Enhancing the computer system to increase the speed of response, and extending the database to give more complete and up to date information	15,000 *
All staff to receive training on the enhanced system, customer care and dealing with enquiries	10,000 *
Employing an additional staff member to attend to enquirers and reduce waiting times	10,000
Refurbishment of the offices, including comfortable seating for those who are waiting	5,000 *
Introduction of a ticket queuing system which allows enquirers to know how long their wait is likely to be	3,000 *
	43,000
Other costs *(comprising mainly of increased management time spent monitoring the use of the new systems and the performance of staff)*	7,000
TOTAL COSTS	**50,000**

* one off costs

The success of the quality initiative will be measured by the change in customer satisfaction ratings, decreasing complaints, along with the quantity and quality of the output from the advice centre.

The quality of this type of service can sometimes be improved with relatively minor changes, e.g. the way in which staff provide information, i.e. with a pleasant manner, a smile, empathy, sympathy etc. This type of quality enhancement may cost nothing in financial terms but still yield increases in customer satisfaction ratings, and decreased complaints.

In the private sector, the cost of quality is sometimes measured in terms of the cost of non-performance and poor quality. This is calculated by considering:

- ❖ The level of penalties incurred (if service under contract)

- ❖ The amount of compensation that needs to be paid (in the event that the service has been negligent)

- ❖ The amount of insurance to be paid (this often increases in line with increased claims arising from poor service)

- ❖ The amount of returns received (in the case of products not being fit for the purpose)

- ❖ The amount of lost custom (resulting from very low satisfaction with the goods or services being provided)

The above approach is also relevant for the public sector.

The fact that poor quality has a cost means that investing in quality enhancement can produce a saving.

Cost of Poor Quality in the Public Sector

- ■ Increased complaints requiring implementation of the complaints procedures, which uses additional staff time.

- Low morale leading to high staff turnover, lost experience and greater need for training new staff, e.g. nurses in the health service

- Correcting errors, e.g. redoing incorrect Council Tax statements

- Generating further enquiries as customers are not satisfied with initial responses, e.g. poor help lines

- Increased legal costs arising from poor services leading to breaches of statutory responsibilities, e.g. some Social Services cases where poor service delivery has led to court cases

- Wasted resources as facilities/services under-utilised as they are so poor, e.g. inhabitable council properties

Benefits of Quality

If there is to be an investment in quality then there has to be some benefits arising from that investment. Benefits can be looked at in two ways:

Tangible Benefits
- Increased service output
- Increased levels of satisfaction
- Reductions in complaints
- Improved working conditions
- Reduced errors/waste

Intangible Benefits
- Reduced stress levels
- Reduced sickness
- Improved staff relations
- Improved customer relations
- Improved public image

Within the public sector there may also be political benefits; the improved image of a service may result in additional votes for local or central government politicians.

In order to compare the benefits with the costs, an organisation needs to be able to translate these benefits into monetary terms. This is often a difficult task, particularly with the intangible benefits. So that this translation can be achieved, there is a need to maintain records with respect to the areas where benefits are expected. These can be very specific, e.g. sickness rates, output volumes, numbers of complaints and so on. Monetary savings can be calculated for these types of benefits in a straight forward manner.

Other areas are more difficult, such as image. An example of translating image into monetary terms is where the image of the public service is so good, users are prepared to pay for it, or pay more. These increased revenues can be attributed to the level of quality, e.g. upgraded leisure centre facilities could result in increased charges being acceptable to the public.

Using the example on page 74 which demonstrated the cost of quality for the advice centre, the benefits of quality could be identified as follows:

In the first year:

	Benefit (£)
Increased satisfaction resulting in less complaints needing to be investigated – saving in staff time	5,000
Increased satisfaction resulting in faster processing time as users are more relaxed, non-aggressive, etc. – saving in staff time	10,000
Reduced waiting times resulting in a reduction of space needed for queuing – saving in office space and overheads	3,000
Provision of more accurate and complete information provided reducing the need for follow-up enquiries – saving in staff time	10,000
Reduced staff sickness rates – saving in time lost due to absence, overtime payments and use of agency staff	5,000
Total Benefit	**33,000 per annum**

In order to arrive at the above figures, it is necessary to have undertaken costing exercises such as the cost per hour of staff and management, the cost per unit of service such as answering an enquiry. With these unit costs it is possible to identify, in monetary terms, the savings resulting from increased quality.

Cost Benefit Analysis

Given that there is a cost to quality and a resulting benefit, it should be possible to make an assessment as to whether the investment in quality is worthwhile. This is usually thought to be the case if the benefits can be shown to outweigh the costs.

Continuing to use the previous advice centre example:

The cost of the quality enhancements to the advice centre can be broken down between one off costs and annual costs as follows:

	Cost (£)
One off costs	33,000
Annual costs	17,000
Total Cost	50,000

The annual benefits are £33,000 (see previous page), therefore the net annual benefit after deduction of the annual costs above are £16,000 (£33,000 – £17,000).

A cost benefit analysis calculation would show that the net annual benefits will cover the one off investment cost in just over 2 years (2 x £16,000). After this point the benefits arising from a higher quality service will outweigh the cost of implementation.

There are other things to consider when undertaking a cost benefit analysis exercise. These include:

❖ Availability of resources/resource limitations

❖ Alternative uses for resources

❖ The cost/implications of not improving quality

❖ Acceptable payback period (some organisations require immediate net benefits)

❖ Organisation's commitment to quality

Quality and Value for Money

In the private sector, quality levels are balanced with demand for the product and the price that the consumer will bear. Therefore quality enhancements can often be passed on to the consumer through the price. In the public sector the relationship is not so clear cut. Often quality has to be balanced with value for money, this is especially important in the current climate of reductions to public spending and user demand for high quality services.

Where public sector services are being tendered, quality standards can be built into service specifications. Then the winning price will be that which determines the best value for money.

Where services are being provided directly by the public sector then value for money is judged by the cost of the service in comparison to the quality of service being delivered. This assessment is made by considering the following:

- ❖ Quality definitions and quality threshold benchmarks
- ❖ Cost comparisons between other public sector providers delivering similar services
- ❖ Comparisons between cost to the public sector for internal delivery and prices charged in the external market for similar services
- ❖ Feedback from service recipients
- ❖ Potential charges that could be made for the service

Value for money will change over time in line with changes in consumer expectations; service delivery methods; relative costs; and the range of service providers. Therefore the organisation has to review value for money on a regular basis to ensure that the relative quality standards being achieved are in line with the cost of the service.

SUMMARY

✧ The cost of quality need not be excessive, and increasing quality can sometimes be achieved at no cost

✧ When establishing the cost of quality, all costs need to be taken into account

✧ Where possible, all costs and benefits of quality improvements should be presented in monetary terms

✧ There are costs associated with not improving quality, such as increased complaints and waste

✧ A cost benefit analysis can be undertaken to help with decisions as to whether or not to invest in a particular quality improvement project

✧ Costs need to be broken down between one-off costs and annual recurring costs. This breakdown should also be undertaken for benefits

✧ Quality has to be balanced with value for money and on occasions, compromises have to be made

Exercise 11

Calculating the Cost of Quality

You have been given the following information:

♦ *Average cost of an employee including on-costs and overheads*   £25,000

♦ *Average direct service delivery days given by employee per annum*   160

♦ *Average number of clients seen per month*   600

♦ *Average time spent with each client per visit (assume that staff can see 3 clients per productive day)*   2 hours

♦ *Average return number of visits required 50% (due to lack of information provided on the first visit)*

♦ *Waiting list 2 months equivalent*

It is recommended that to enhance quality, the average visit times be increased by 10 minutes, resulting in the need for an extra 200 days staff time per annum with the following consequences:

♦ *Impact on staff time would be to increase staff numbers by 1.25 FTEs*

♦ *Impact on return visits required would be to reduce them to 25%*

♦ *Impact on waiting list would be to reduce it down to the equivalent of 1 month*

Calculate the current cost of the service

£

Calculate the cost of the quality improvement

£

State two simple ways of reducing the above cost(s)

(i)

(ii)

Suggested solutions to this exercise can be found on page 126.

Exercise 12

Cost/Benefit Analysis

Take a service where you work or are very familiar with and identify a potential improvement that could be made to enhance service quality.

Complete the following:

Service Description:

Cost of Quality Improvement

	£
e.g. *Additional staff time*	_____
Additional training	_____
Additional equipment	_____
Improved environment	_____
Other _____	_____
_____	_____
_____	_____
_____	_____
_____	_____
_____	_____
TOTAL COST	£ _____ **A**

Estimate the potential monetary value of the benefits to be derived from the quality improvements.

Benefits

	£
e.g. reduced staff sickness and less staff turnover (hence less recruitment costs/time) improved, morale (better productivity), etc.	
_____	_____
_____	_____
_____	_____
_____	_____
_____	_____

TOTAL BENEFITS	£ _____	**B**

Having calculated both the cost and the benefit, undertake some cost benefit analysis

NET COST/BENEFIT   *(A - B)*   £ _____

PAY BACK PERIOD $\dfrac{B}{A}$ £ _____

Given the above, do you think your idea for quality improvement is worth while?

Yes .... ☐

No .... ☐

Yes with modifications .... ☐

Chapter 7

OBTAINING RECOGNISED QUALITY STANDARDS

To facilitate the process of developing quality systems, recognised quality standards are often applied. These include charter marks, ISO9000, ISO14000, (environmental quality management systems), Investors In People, and so on. None of these standards conflict with each other, however, each service area should consider which will be most beneficial in achieving their quality goals. In the following paragraphs we discuss the most popular quality kite marks:

⇨ **ISO 9000**

⇨ **Investors In People (IIP)**

⇨ **Charter Mark**

ISO 9000

ISO 9000 is an internationally recognised quality standard for management systems. It is not unusual for tenders to specify ISO 9000 as a requirement, or that the standard should be achieved within a certain amount of time.

ISO9000 consists of several parts applicable to different types of services; the most widely used is ISO9002. This relates to production and delivery services; other parts include ISO9001 covering design and ISO9003 which applies to services whose quality can only be gained by inspection.

ISO9000 verifies that the defined quality and standards of service which are said to be provided are in fact provided. This is achieved by:

- ❖ Full documentation of the processes and procedures involved in service delivery, along with the quality policies

- ❖ Identification of where measures/checks are taken

- ❖ Verification by way of audit to ensure that procedures are followed

- ❖ Documentation of all non-conforming services along with a full investigation

- ❖ External verification

The structure of ISO9000 concentrates on four main elements:

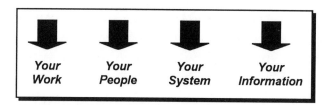

| **Your Work** | **Your People** | **Your System** | **Your Information** |

There are 20 parts to the standard which need to be achieved for ISO9000. These are set out in the following diagram.

A Summary of the standard

Your Work

Eleven clauses in ISO9000 govern the work you do. The work clauses start when you receive an order or an enquiry, and finish at the moment you deliver the finished product or service. The clauses are:

- *Purchasing*
- *Contract Review*
- *Customer Supplied Product*
- *Design Control*
- *Process Control*
- *Testing (3 clauses)*
- *Control of Non-Conforming Product*
- *Handling, Storage, Packaging and Delivery*
- *Servicing*

Your People	**Your System**	**Your Information**
Two clauses relate to your staff. The clauses ask you to manage staff in such a way that everyone knows what is going on.	Four clauses cover the quality system. They make sure you carry out audits and control key documents, so that your organisation will run smoothly.	Three clauses make sure that your decisions are based on solid information. They ask you to identify your products and keep records.
◆ *Management Responsibility* ◆ *Training*	◆ *Quality System* ◆ *Document Control* ◆ *Corrective Action* ◆ *Internal Quality Audits*	◆ *Product Identification* ◆ *Records* ◆ *Statistical Techniques*

(Adapted from ISO 9000/BS5750 Made Easy)

The advantages gained by public sector service providers obtaining this standard are summarised as follows:

❖ Ensures all aspects of service delivery are documented, and hence requires thought about exactly what the service is, how it is delivered, and the standards that need to be achieved

❖ Provides a framework for regular auditing of the system and hence more effective monitoring

❖ Requires services to be delivered in a consistent manner at all times

❖ Gives more credibility to quality assertions made when tendering for work

❖ May give confidence to the customer/user that the published standards for service delivery have been validated

❖ Provides an opportunity for an independent assessor to establish that the quality system and supporting processes and procedures are in place, and operational

In attempting to attain and maintain ISO9000, there are a number of potential difficulties that need to be taken into account. These are:

❖ It may be expensive as certification has to be paid for

❖ It may be very time consuming, particularly for services that do not already have some systems in place

❖ It concentrates on the existing service and how it is delivered (which does not necessarily mean that the service currently reaches the required standard)

❖ There is no need to involve third parties in the process, e.g. the service users

❖ It may result in a great deal of increased paper work and unnecessary bureaucracy

❖ Some staff may find it too rigid given the nature of the service, resulting in a loss of creativity and an inability to use professional discretion where necessary

These difficulties can be overcome, but it should be remembered that ISO9000 does not mean a "high quality" service is being delivered. It only shows that the service conforms to documented procedures. It cannot be used to compare the service delivered by one organisation with another as both could have ISO9000 but deliver very different quality services.

Investors in People

This is an international award which looks at how people are utilised in the achievement of organisational objectives and covers the following:

❖ Business plan and objectives communicated to staff

❖ Job descriptions

❖ Induction

❖ Appraisal

❖ Training and development

❖ Evaluation

There are four principles which define whether or not an organisation is an investor in people. In order to help an organisation assess whether or not it meets those principles there are twenty three indicators, which are set out in the following paragraphs.

Principle One: Commitment

An investor in people makes a commitment from the top to develop all employees to achieve its business objectives

1.1 The commitment from top management to train and develop employees is effectively communicated throughout the organisation

1.2 Employees at all levels are aware of the broad aims or vision of the organisation

1.3 The organisation has considered what employees at all levels will contribute to the success of the organisation, and has effectively communicated this to them

1.4 Where representative structures exist, communication takes place between management and representatives on the vision of where the organisation is going and the contribution employees (and their representatives) will make to its success

Principle Two: Planning

An investor in people regularly reviews the needs and plans the training and development of all employees

2.1 A written but flexible plan sets out the organisation's goals and targets

2.2 A written plan identifies the organisation's training and development needs, and specifies what actions will be taken to meet these needs

2.3 Training and development needs are regularly reviewed against goals and targets at the organisation, team and individual level

2.4 A written plan identifies the resources that will be used to meet training and development needs

2.5 Responsibility for training and developing employees is clearly identified and understood throughout the organisation starting at the top

2.6 Objectives are set for training and development actions at the organisation, team and individual level

2.7 Where appropriate, training and development objectives are linked to external standards, such as National Vocational Qualifications (NVQs) or Scottish Vocational Qualifications (SVQs) and units

---

Principle Three: *Action*

An Investor in people takes action to train and develop individuals on recruitment and throughout their employment

3.1 All new employees are effectively introduced to the organisation and all employees new to a job are given the training and development they need to perform that job

3.2 Managers are effective in carrying out their responsibilities for training and developing employees

3.3 Managers are actively involved in supporting employees to meet their training and development needs

3.4 All employees are made aware of the training and development opportunities open to them

3.5 All employees are encouraged to help identify and meet their job-related training and development needs

3.6 Action takes place to meet the training and development needs of individuals, teams and the organisation

Principle Four: ***Evaluation***

An investor in people evaluates the investment in training and development to assess achievement and improve future effectiveness

4.1 The organisation evaluates the impact of training and development actions on knowledge, skills and attitude

4.2 The organisation evaluates the impact of training and development actions on performance

4.3 The organisation evaluates the contribution of training and development to the achievement of its goals and targets

4.4 Top management understands the broad cost and benefits of training and developing employees

4.5 Action takes place to implement improvements to training and development identified as a result of evaluation

4.6 Top management's continuing commitment to training and developing employees is demonstrated to all employees

(Investors in People UK 1997)

The advantages of IIP in the public sector can be summarised as follows:

❖ It can apply to every type of service within the public sector because it focuses on people

❖ It provides a framework to bring together many of the activities already taking place within the organisation

❖ It provides an action plan to fill the gaps that may exist within the areas of development and training

❖ It should provide a morale boost for staff at all levels and result in greater productivity and commitment

❖ It should result in better planning and improved communication throughout the organisation

❖ It can be used as a catalyst for change, especially addressing areas such as attitude and commitment to organisational goals

There may be potential difficulties with IIP and these are summarised as follows:

❖ May be expensive and is most definitely time consuming if done properly

❖ Some believe it to be a paper exercise and not translated into real action for the staff (verifiers do try and check that this is not the case)

❖ It has an inward focus and does not take into account views from third parties, such as service users

❖ Obtaining participation and involvement of all staff may prove difficult without proper coordination

As with ISO9000 these difficulties can be overcome with proper planning and real commitment from the top of the organisation.

Comparisons between ISO9000 and IIP

When looking at the two quality standards, it should be emphasised that they are complementary and not conflicting.

IIP	ISO9000
• International – All organisations hope to meet assessment criteria.	• Individual – In so far as it recognises that an organisation has a system in place that it adheres to. However, the system is not benchmarked in any way and cannot be used as a comparison.
• Concentrates on people and their contribution to achieving organisational objectives.	• Concentrates on systems to ensure that the product/service consistently meets set standards.
• Ideal for service businesses which are very dependent on people for the delivery of services.	• Ideal for manufacturing companies that depend on effective systems to ensure products have zero defects.

Where possible, organisations should <u>seek</u> to attain both standards, as each can benefit the development of a quality centred organisation.

Charter Mark

"Service First" is the Charter programme which aims to improve service delivery across the public sector. It gives an emphasis on promoting responsiveness, quality effectiveness, and cross-sectoral working.

There are ten principles of public service delivery which every public service should be striving to achieve, these are set out as follows:

1. **Set Standards of Service**

   Set clear standards of service that users can expect; monitor and review performance; and publish the results, following independent validation wherever possible

2. **Be Open and Provide Full Information**

   Be open and communicate clearly and effectively in plain language, to help people using public services and provide full information about services, their cost and how well they perform

3. **Consult and Involve**

   Consult and involve present and potential users of public services, as well as those who work in them; and use their views to improve the service provided

4. **Encourage Access and the Promotion of Choice**

   Make services easily available to everyone who needs them, including using technology to the full and offering choice wherever possible

5. **Treat all Fairly**

   Treat all people fairly; respect their privacy and dignity; be helpful and courteous; and pay particular attention to those with special needs

6. **Put Things Right When They go Wrong**

   Put things right quickly and effectively; learn from complaints; and have a clear, well publicised, and easy-to-use complaints procedure, with independent review wherever possible

7. **Use Resources Effectively**

   Use resources effectively to provide best value for taxpayers and users

8. **Innovate and Improve**

   Always look for ways to improve the services and facilities offered

9. Work with Other Providers

Work with other providers to ensure that services are simple to use, effective and coordinated, and deliver a better service to the user

10. User Satisfaction

Show that your users are satisfied with the quality of service they are receiving

A Charter Mark is the UK Government's award scheme for recognising and encouraging excellence in the public service. To win a Charter Mark, organisations must demonstrate excellence against the criteria given.

Unlike ISO9000 and IIP which are generally awarded to organisations as a whole, a Charter Mark can be awarded to a specific service, which may be only part of the organisation's activities. The Charter Mark has a particular focus on service delivery to the user and getting user involvement and satisfaction, unlike the others that tend to focus on processes and systems within the organisation.

All three of the above do have things in common:

❖ They are all assessed independently by external bodies

❖ The awards are usually difficult to obtain

❖ All expect continuous quality improvement

❖ If the award is achieved it has to be regularly audited

❖ The award is not automatically renewed, and can be taken away if standards have not been maintained

All of these recognitions of quality are complementary to each other and there is no reason why an organisation should not seek to obtain them all.

SUMMARY

✧ ISO9000 concentrates on management systems and has 20 parts to the standard that need to be achieved. These cover 'your work', 'your systems', 'your people' and 'your information'

✧ There are four principles that define an Investor in People, these are Commitment, Planning, Action and Evaluation. An Investor in People ensures everyone understands how they contribute to the achievement of organisational objectives

✧ The Charter Mark focuses on individual services and places emphasis on customer feedback and satisfaction (areas not covered with ISO9000 and IIP)

✧ All quality standards are worth while, however, each organisation must assess which are the most relevant to their development as a quality organisation delivering quality services

Exercise 13

Do You Meet the Standard?

Complete the following questionnaire in relation to your service/ organisation. Tick yes, no or partly in relation to each question.

ISO 9000	Yes	Partly	No
1. Do you have a policy with respect to quality and what it means for the service/organisation?			
2. Do all staff delivering the service understand the quality policy?			
3. Is there a person with specific responsibility for quality?			
4. Is there a senior manager with specific responsibility for quality?			
5. Does the senior management team discuss quality on a regular basis at team meetings?			
6. Are there written instructions with respect to how services should be delivered (i.e. quality manuals)?			
7. Do these instructions cover all areas from inputs to outcomes, as well as details of the process?			
8. Are there standards developed for each aspect of service delivery?			
9. Are there performance indicators for each aspect of these standards?			
10. Are performance indicators measured and monitored on a regular basis?			
11. Is there a quality plan in existence setting out what needs to be done and how quality will be monitored and continuously improved?			
12. Is there a co-ordinated procedure for collecting, collating and feeding back information on quality attainment?			

	Yes	Partly	No
13. Do you maintain a file of quality records?			
14. Are there regular quality audits and audit reports?			
15. Are exceptions to quality standards investigated and resolved?			
16. Are exceptions to quality standards regularly reported and shared with staff?			
17. Are quality manuals updated on a regular basis, and staff inducted on the updates?			
18. Is there a staff training plan?			
19. Do staff receive regular training?			
20. Are you happy with the administration in respect of all aspects of the service (includes record keeping, filing, accuracy, completeness etc.)?			

Complete the following questionnaire in relation to your service/organisation. Tick yes, no or partly in relation to each question.

Investors in People	Yes	Partly	No
1. Has there been a commitment from the top of the organisation (or service) to becoming an Investor in People?			
2. Is there a business plan in existence?			
3. Do all staff know and understand the objectives of the service/organisation?			
4. Is there an objective in respect of staff training and development?			
5. Are all staff aware of who is responsible for training and development?			
6. Have specific resources been set aside for staff training and development (financial, physical, and time)?			
7. Are staff encouraged to acquire recognised qualifications?			
8. Do staff show a willingness to participate in training?			
9. Is there a comprehensive induction process?			
10. Are managers involved in the training and development of their staff?			
11. Are managers assessed on their ability to train and develop their staff?			
12. Is there an appraisal system that covers all levels of staff?			
13. Does the appraisal system identify training needs?			
14. Are staff encouraged to request training for their own or team development?			

	Yes	Partly	No
15. Are there any incentives for staff if they undergo training?			
16. Is there a regular review of training needs for the organisation as a whole?			
17. Is there a monitoring system in place to assess the impact of training?			
18. Is training discussed with staff before they participate in it, to ensure that it is appropriate to their needs and to identify the expected outcomes as a result of the training?			
19. Is the outcome of training assessed after six months in order to identify whether or not there has been an impact on job performance and the achievement of service/ organisational objectives?			
20. Is the training evaluation data used to update business plans and training plans?			

Suggested solutions to this exercise can be found on page 128.

Chapter 8

IMPLEMENTING QUALITY

Difficulties and Solutions

The practical side of implementing effective quality systems is often fraught with difficulties, and many public sector organisations have an uphill task when trying to become a "quality organisation". Some of the most common difficulties have been identified below:

- ❖ Lack of financial and physical resources

- ❖ Lack of expertise around quality issues

- ❖ Historically poor service delivery in some areas and lack of benchmarks against which to set quality improvements

- ❖ Low quality image ingrained in the minds of the consumer/public

- ❖ Low morale amongst staff and few ways of providing incentives

Some practical solutions that may solve these difficulties include:

❖ Obtaining external funds from organisations that support quality initiatives, such as Training and Enterprise Councils (TECs) who are often prepared to help organisations to achieve Investors in People

❖ Where possible, ensuring that quality improvements are self-financing , i.e. quantifiable savings can be made as a result of the changes introduced

❖ Having a timetable for quality improvements which allows costs to be spread over a number of years, but which does not become disjointed leading to fragmentation in the quality process

❖ Getting volunteers to assist with environmental development projects

❖ Through training and development, changing the culture within the organisation to reflect the level of service quality required

❖ Undertaking in-house, on-the-job training on issues that will promote quality such as customer care, telephone manner, dealing with the public, service knowledge and so on.

❖ Letting staff develop their own quality procedures, and manuals

❖ Working with organisations that have already implemented quality initiatives and learning from their successes and failures

❖ Using best practice guides produced by the Cabinet Office's, Service First new charter programme to assist in quality implementation, e.g. "How to conduct written consultation exercises". There are also quality networks that have been set up by the Cabinet Office (22 in the UK to date). These networks have managers from a wide range of public service providers who meet to exchange ideas on quality issues and provide information.

❖ Developing quality definitions and standards which involve everyone, using the starting point of "what makes the service satisfactory for the users, staff and the organisation"

❖ Establishing a marketing campaign that promotes the organisation's attitude to quality and the changes that are being made. This should include details of the quality standards for the service, in a way that the public appreciate and understand

❖ Ensuring that some of the quality enhancements are physically noticeable to the consumer, and a pro-active approach is taken in developing advocates for the service

❖ Promoting positive feedback received by staff and giving praise at every opportunity

❖ Giving staff awards for being successful in the way they promote quality and deliver quality services to the public

An example of how central government departments are trying to become more focused on quality is demonstrated by the development of six new standards referred to as the "Whitehall standards".

The Six Whitehall Standards

**In serving you, every central government department
and agency will aim to do the following:**

1. Answer your letters quickly and clearly. Each department and agency will set a target for answering letters and will publish its performance against this target. (Note: Currently response time targets vary from 10 days - HM Customs and Excise, to 20 days - Department of Health)

2. See you within 10 minutes of any appointment you have made at its office

3. Provide clear and straightforward information about its services and at least one number for telephone enquiries to help you or to put you in touch with someone else

4. Consult its users regularly about the services it provides and report on the results

5. Have at least one complaints procedure for the services it provides, and send you information about a procedure if you ask

6. Do everything that is reasonably possible to make its services available to everyone, including people with special needs

---

Performance against these standards will be measured and published such that they can be judged by the public.

Key Steps

The key steps to effective quality implementation can be summarised as follows:

- ❖ Commitment to quality must come from the top and be ongoing, i.e. not a one off project

- ❖ Ensure quality improvement programmes are not confused with cost-cutting/savings initiatives

- ❖ Staff are involved throughout the whole process of quality development, with leadership coming from the top and detailed implementation from the bottom-up

- ❖ Customers, users, stakeholders, and the public need to be involved throughout the process with constant consultation and feedback

- ❖ Continual training and development around areas of quality throughout the process of implementation and afterwards

- ❖ Understand that quality does not stand still and therefore the organisation needs to be striving for continuous improvement in all areas

- ❖ Each year standards need to be made public along with the results of the measurement and monitoring

- ❖ Realistic timetables need to be set such that quality can really be achieved and not be superficial. This may take a number of years to ensure a quality culture is embedded throughout the organisation

It should be remembered that every organisation is different and therefore the solution to implementing quality will be different in each case.

Exercise 14

Action Plan

Thinking about all the areas of the book:

⇨ What is Quality?

⇨ Setting Quality Standards

⇨ Measuring and Monitoring Quality

⇨ Quality Management

⇨ Investing in Quality

⇨ Obtaining Recognised Quality Standards

⇨ Implementing Quality

Consider what actions need to be taken in order to improve your service in each of these areas, and what actions you personally intend to take

	How can my service area improve?	*What actions can I take?*
What is Quality?		

	How can my service area improve?	What actions can I take?
Setting Quality Standards		
Measuring and Monitoring Quality		
Quality Management		

	How can my service area improve?	What actions can I take?
Investing in Quality?		
Obtaining Recognised Quality Standards		
Implementing Quality		

SOLUTIONS
TO
EXERCISES

Solutions to Exercises

Solution to Exercise 1
Values and Objectives
~ Impact on Quality ~

For the following example, set out what you consider to be:

a) *The most important values*

b) *The key strategic objectives*

c) *The impact on quality*

A person who buys a Rolls Royce	*A person who buys a Lada*
VALUES: ● *Reliability* ● *Investment* ● *Durability* ● *Safety* ● *Image*	*VALUES:* ● *Economy* ● *Practicality*
OBJECTIVES: ● *To own a high specification car that holds its value and projects an image*	*OBJECTIVES:* ● *To own a vehicle that gets one from A to B in a cost effective manner*
IMPACT ON QUALITY: ● *Expecting zero defects, high performance, and a high level of customer care*	*IMPACT ON QUALITY:* ● *No surprise if there are a few problems*

Solution to Exercise 2
Service Quality Definitions

Public Sector Values

1) *Value for money*

2) *Community*

3) *Environment*

4) *Efficiency*

5) *Equality*

Quality Definition Example

> A value for money, and environmentally friendly bus service for **all** the community

Private Sector Values

1) *Profit*
2) *Efficiency*
3) *Cost Effectiveness*
4) *Customer Care*
5) *Image*

Quality Definition Example

> A cost effective and profitable school bus service that meets our customers' requirements

Solution to Exercise 4
Quality Standards

Insert your public sector definition for the School Bus Service from Exercise 2, then set a number of quality standards that you would be prepared to put on show to the general public.

Quality Definition

A value for money, and environmentally friendly bus service for all the community

---

Quality Standards

Tangible:

➭ Keeping within x minutes of the time table

➭ Achieving average journey times between stops

➭ Achieving minimum waiting times for passengers at stops

➭ Visiting all schools on the route

➭ Keeping vehicles maintained and below a certain age

Intangible:

➭ Pleasant and clean environment on the bus

➭ Polite and helpful drivers

➭ Customer satisfaction rating of x%

➭ Implementing equal opportunities policies

Solution to Exercise 6
Performance Indicators

For each standard identified in Exercise 4, list at least two performance indicators (think about how they might be measured).

Standard	Performance Indicators	Measurement
Keeping within x minutes of the timetable	*Times of arrival at the stop*	*Time log – daily*
	Times of departure from the stop	*Time log – daily*
Achieving average journey times between stops	*Times of departure from one stop*	*Time log – daily*
	Times of arrival at the following stop	*Time log – daily*
Achieving minimum waiting times for passengers at stops	*Times between buses arriving at each stop*	*Time log – daily*
	Passenger feedback on their waiting time	*Customer/user survey – every six months*
Visiting all schools on the route	*Time of arrival at each stop*	*Time log – daily*
	Feedback from schools on the route	*Schools survey – every six months*

Standard	Performance Indicators	Measurement
Keeping vehicles maintained and below a certain age	*Number of breakdowns*	*Record of each breakdown and the impact immediately logged in breakdown book*
	Age of vehicles	*Date of vehicle purchase for all vehicles in use*
Pleasant and clean environment	*Litter levels*	*Bus inspection – daily*
	Feedback from users	*Customer/user survey – every six months*
Polite and helpful driver	*Number of complaints*	*No. of complaints registered in complaints book – each month*
	Feedback from users	*Customer/user survey – every six months*
Customer satisfaction rating of x%	*Number of complaints*	*No. of complaints registered in complaints book – each month*
	Feedback from users	*Customer/user survey – every six months*
Implementing equal opportunities policies	*Number of complaints*	*No. of complaints registered in complaints book – each month*
	Feedback from users	*Customer/user survey – every six months*

Solution to Exercise 7
Measuring Performance

Given the scenarios provided, note down the following for each case.

> ### a) Is this a quality Service?
>
> **Case 1**
> *Yes, in the eyes of the provider. No, in the eyes of the customer; therefore for a customer focused organisation, the answer should be no.*
>
> **Case 2**
> *Yes, as the specification is met and the specification sets the quality definitions and standards.*
>
> **Case 3**
> *Unclear because the service manager appears to be content with the service and only has the view of one employee. Further investigation would need to take place in order to establish the position. However, certain practices, if true, would be considered poor.*

> ### b) What type of performance measurement would you undertake?
>
> **Case 1**
> *Accuracy and customer satisfaction survey.*
>
> **Case 2**
> *Inspection of rubbish levels between emptying times, and local resident satisfaction survey.*
>
> **Case 3**
> *Real waiting times, i.e. when someone gets seen, and customer satisfaction survey.*

c) How could the service be improved?

Case 1 Better consultation with the customer (managers) to establish what they consider the quality standards ought to be. Develop the service quality accordingly.

Case 2 Evaluation of the specification in the light of local feedback from satisfaction surveys and complaints. Revised specification for next tendering round to reflect the evaluation results.

Case 3 Ensuring all staff are adequately trained and adhering to a quality manual which sets out clearly how each aspect of the service should be delivered in order to meet the quality standards. Closer monitoring by the manager, and evaluation of customer feedback/satisfaction with the overall service.

Solution to Exercise 9
Total Quality Management in Practice

Some of the actions the manager could undertake to develop a TQM system are given below (note these are not in any order of priority)

- ➢ Produce a mission statement
- ➢ Introduce staff appraisals and performance management
- ➢ Select a TQM team including staff and representation from users
- ➢ Paint the common parts and recover furniture
- ➢ Introduce procedures manuals for all areas of work, setting standards, targets and monitoring procedures
- ➢ Change current caterers, currently sub-contractors, and issue new guidelines on menus
- ➢ Set out objectives for the next five years which identify quality improvements
- ➢ Make a commitment to becoming an Investor in People
- ➢ Develop a corporate logo and use throughout the organisation
- ➢ Introduce activities such as film making, fitness training, and an educational programme
- ➢ Undertake a satisfaction survey amongst users and ask for suggested improvements
- ➢ Undertake a staff survey and ask for suggested improvements
- ➢ Undertake a visitors survey and ask for improvements

- Implement a staff training programme
- Develop regular meetings with users and visitors
- Make the visiting areas more comfortable, include new drinks machine, etc.
- Obtain ISO 9002 accreditation
- Have regular staff meetings
- Appoint a new independent person to deal with complaints and to audit quality systems
- Have an annual open day

Solution to Exercise 11
Calculating the Cost of Quality

You have been given the following information:

- *Average cost of an employee including on-costs and overheads* £25,000

- *Average direct service delivery days given by employee per annum* 160

- *Average number of clients seen per month* 600

- *Average time spent with each client per visit (assume that staff can see 3 clients per productive day)* 2 hours

- *Average return number of visits required 50% (due to lack of information provided on the first visit)*

- *Waiting list 2 months equivalent*

It is recommended that to enhance quality, the average visit times be increased by 10 minutes, resulting in the need for an extra 200 days staff time per annum

- *Impact on staff time would be to increase staff numbers by 1.25 FTEs*

- *Impact on return visits required would be to reduce them to 25%*

- *Impact on waiting list would be to reduce it down to 1 month equivalent*

The current cost of the service (staff only)   £375,000*

* *200 productive days per month required to see 600 clients per month, because only 3 clients can be seen in one productive staff day.*

200 x 12 = 2,400 productive days per annum required to see all the clients.

Each staff member currently delivers 160 productive days per annum.

Therefore, it will take 15 staff members to deliver the 2,400 days (2,400 ÷ 160)

The cost is therefore £375,000 (15 x 25,000)

The cost of the quality improvement   £31,250**

** *(£25,000 x 1.25)*

Two simple ways of reducing the above cost of quality:

(i) Increase the number of direct delivery days worked by each member of staff by 14 days per year to 174 days. This would absorb the extra 200 days required without extra staff costs.

(ii) Review the way in which the service is being delivered and consider alternative ways. For example, using technology may lead to greater efficiency and yield an opportunity for reducing costs.

Solution to Exercise 13

Do You Meet the Standard?

Award yourself the following points for each question:

Yes	=	2 points
Partly	=	1 point
No	=	nil points

ISO 9000

Points scored: Under 20

Although this is a low score it does not mean that the service being delivered is of poor quality. The score reflects the lack of formalisation in the way in which services are currently delivered, along with a general lack of documentation and record keeping. It may be that your service does not lend itself well to structures, and systems. However, there is merit at trying to at least put in place some of the key elements required for ISO 9000, such as service standards and procedure manuals, even if you consider that achieving the standard is not appropriate for your service/ organisation.

Points Scored: 20 to 29

This is an average score, and not surprising for many public service providers who have not fully embarked on the path to becoming a quality organisation. This score indicates that there are elements in existence that can be used to help in the development of a quality system, and hence provide a starting point for ISO 9000. The next stage is to prepare a comprehensive action plan identifying where the gaps are and how these can be filled. This may take some time, and if ISO 9000 is a goal then your service/ organisation should have a realistic timetable for its achievement, at least a year.

Points Scored: 30 to 40

This score indicates that you should have very little difficulty in preparing for ISO 9000. However, if you have not scored yes to questions 6 to 10 and number 17 there may still be a lot of work to be done in order to be confident that you are adequately prepared to be assessed for the standard. Even if you do not wish to go through the process of gaining accreditation it is still worthwhile aiming to eliminate any no answers such that you can be assured you have the system in place to achieve the level of quality desired by your service/organisation.

INVESTORS IN PEOPLE

You may find that your scores are very different to the previous self assessment results for ISO 9000. This may affect which standard you wish to achieve first.

Points Scored: Under 20

Given that staff are very important to the delivery of most public sector services, this is a low score that needs to be addressed even if your service/organisation does not wish to acquire the standard. As a matter of good practice there should be certain basic processes in place such as appraisals and training plans. It is unlikely that staff will perform to the best of their abilities if no effort is being put into their training and development. It makes good sense in terms of quality and value for money to ensure that you strive to meet the under pinning principles of IIP, whereby investing in staff is linked to the achievement of organisational goals.

Points Scored: 20 to 29

This is an average score, and indicates that there may be some fundamental elements missing from the current organisation's training and development processes. This may be in the area of business planning, where staff are not aware of the organisation's objectives and the contribution they should be making towards their achievement, or it may mean that there is no appraisal system in place for all staff. If you do have gaps of this nature then there will be a reasonable amount of work required to meet the standard and hence a realistic time scale needs to be adopted for its achievement, at least a year.

Points Scored: 30 to 40

This score indicates that you have most of the required processes in place in order to become an Investor in People. This is not to say that when you prepare your action plan there will not be things that need to be done. Most organisations in your position find evaluation to be the most difficult area to address. Although training and development is well established, the impact of it is often not thoroughly tested and examined. If this is a weak area it may be worth investing in some assistance in identifying the most appropriate method of evaluating training for your service/ organisation.

INDEX

INDEX

A

Action plans 44, 45
Appraisal systems 58
Appraisals 91
Auditing systems 44, 61, 62, 90
Audits 66, 88

B

Benchmark 21, 31, 42, 105
Benefits of quality 76, 77
Best practice 106
Business plan 44, 91
Business planning cycle 57

C

Central Government 1
Certification 90
Charter marks 87, 96
Codes of practice 60
Communication
  Internal and external 12
Communication methods 8
Consumer attitudes 6, 62, 105
Consumer expectations 21, 62
Consumer surveys 62
Continuous improvement 43
Cost benefit analysis 78
Cost of quality 71, 82. *See also* Resources

D

Defining quality 4, 24
Definitions of quality 3
Developing standards 25
Direct costs 73

E

Employee attitudes 7
Employee expectations 21, 59
External influences 6

F

Focus groups 62

I

Indirect costs 73
Input standards 26
Intangible quality standards 22, 31, 37, 46
Internal/external communication 11
Investors in People 91, 106
  Advantages 94
  Comparison with ISO9000 96
  Difficulties 95
ISO9000 65, 88
  Advantages 90
  Comparison with IIP 96
  Difficulties 90

K

Kite marks 87

L

M

O

P

Q

Qualitative 38, 46
  Standards 61
Quality auditor 63
Quality circles 59
Quality definition 30, 31, 62, 80, 107
Quality framework 11, 23
Quality manuals 61, 88, 106
  Flow charts 61
Quality organisation 57, 59
Quality policy and procedures 11, 44, 88
Quality standards 2, 22, 31, 43, 59, 62
Quality systems
  Difficulties in implementation 105
  Implementation 105
Quantitative 38, 46
  Standards 61

R

Recognised quality standards 87
Resources 22, 26, 29, 40, 43, 71, 79, 95, 105

S

Service developments 43
"Service First" 96
Service quality 9
Setting standards 45
Strategic objectives 5

T

Tangible quality standards 22, 28, 31, 37, 46
Target setting 45
Targets for performance 42, 58
 Maintaining 43
Timetable 106
Total quality management 55
Training and Enterprise Council 91, 106

V

Value for money 80, 82

W

Whitehall standards 107, 108